The Winding Road

W. Edmund Hood

Ung Ho Chang

LLUMINA ☆ STARS

Requests for permission to make copies of any part of this work should be mailed to Permissions Department, Llumina Stars, PO Box 772246, Coral Springs, FL 33077-2246

ISBN: 978-1-93362-639-0

Printed in the United States of America by Llumina Stars

Library of Congress Control Number: 2008910463

The Winding Road

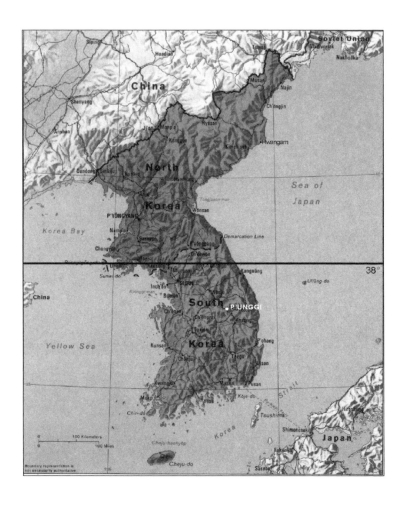

Source: Library of Congress

Chapter 1

The Road Begins

I am Ung Ho Chang. I was born Korean; I am an American. The road from one to the other has been a long one with many rough spots, unexpected turns, and by-ways leading off in the wrong direction. On the road of life, one cannot see beyond the next turn or over the next hill. There are many surprises, and not all are pleasant. I wish to tell you of my journey along that road, so that you may better know what a good thing we Americans have, and what many of us must endure before we can achieve it.

The road began on August 28, 1930, in the Korean town of P'unggi, about 150 miles southeast of Seoul. I was the second youngest of nine children. When I began taking lessons at the schoolmaster's house in P'unggi, there was no way I could see the road that lay ahead of me. It was just as well that I at least enjoyed childhood before having to deal with the terror of flight from war, my brief career as a spy, the betrayals and my internment in a POW camp of the very people for whom I had spied.

Korea was very different then from the way it is today. Attached to a corner of Southeast Asia like a geographical afterthought, it was called by some, "The Land of the Morning Calm." Her people dressed in white – men and women, young and old, everybody wore white, a color that to those in neighboring China symbolized mourning. To us it was what we wore, that's all. Like anybody else, we tended our shops and tilled our fields. Our children played their games, helped out at home, or went to school. When the wars let us be, we were a quiet people with a gentle way of life, and we liked it that way.

The village in which I grew up was similar to this one.
(Photo by E. M. Newman, prior to 1923, from the
Library of Congress.)

Typical Korean gentlemen before the temple of the God of War, Seoul, Korea. Copyright 1904 by Underwood & Underwood

Everybody customarily dressed in white.
(Photo from an old stereo picture in the Library of Congress.)

When the wars let us be, we were a quiet people with a gentle
way of life, and we liked it that way.
(From U.S. Army Historic Collection Online.)

(From U.S. Army Historic Collection Online.)

My family were farmers. We lived in the town, but the fields where we farmed were a mile or two away. P'unggi was situated at a crossroads, which divided the town into four boroughs, or dongs. The main roads were lined with shops, and there were many side roads leading into the dongs. Each dong contained about 300 households, and had several public wells. The head officer of the town, equivalent to the mayor in this country, was called the Myen Chang, and his administration was always under the close scrutiny of the Japanese police, as our land was ruled by Japan in those days.

I lived in the southeastern dong. Our house was made of bamboo framework plastered with clay, and the roof was thatched with rice straw. It had one story, consisting of four rooms and a kitchen, arranged in an L shape. There were no windows, just doors. Furniture was sparse, and very simple. We ate our meals sitting on the floor at low tables. At night, we slept on mats spread out on the floor. By day, most of our activity was outside, except during the wintertime.

Heating in the wintertime was achieved by a wood fire set in a pit, well below floor level, in one corner of the room. Smoke from the fire was channeled through a space beneath the floor to the chimney, which was in the opposite corner. The flooring, being made of slate covered with clay, retained the heat from the smoke. With the heat coming from the floor beneath us, and with warm blankets covering us, we were kept warm all night, even in the coldest of times. It was an ingenious and effective system, but so simple to build that every home, rich or poor, had one.

Electricity and running water in our homes were unheard of in the 1930's. Human and animal waste was carried away in buckets slung from a yoke on the shoulders, to the fields a mile or two away, where it was spread out and combined with the soil as fertilizer. We got our water for drinking and washing from a public well, and lighting came from oil lamps consisting of small containers of oil, each one with a wick sticking out of the cover, and set on a pedestal.

We had a modest, simple diet, consisting mostly of food that we grew ourselves and meat purchased from local vendors. There was the rice from our field, as well as potatoes and other vegetables, many of which we preserved as kim chi. Kim chi has always been an important Korean staple. Since electricity and refrigeration were not available, we kept our food cool by putting it into large, earthen jars sunk into the ground, in a well-shaded place. Cut up vegetables were put into such a jar, salt and spices were added, and the mixture was stirred periodically. The resulting concoction was either eaten directly or cooked. It could be served up as soup, or in as many variations as the imagination might conceive.

We farmed two tiny fields, a mile or two away from home. One was a rice paddy, about 1 acre, which we rented for 30% of the crop. The other, our vegetable garden, was a piece of ground about a half acre in size, belonging to a wealthy person who lived far from the town. It contained the graves of his parents, and we were allowed to farm the ground in exchange for our taking care of the grave site and leaving an annual offering of food on the graves. My parents hadn't heard from him in a long time, but they kept tending the grave site.

The weeks preceding harvest were often the most difficult. It was then that food was scarcest, and we often had to make do with whatever was available, or go hungry. I remember one day when my mother told me to go out to the rice paddy and bring some home for dinner. "Mom," I said, "It's not ripe yet. It's still green. How can we eat it?"

"Go get it anyway," she told me, "and I'll show you how."

I went out to the paddy and got three bundles of the unripe rice which I brought home. It didn't seem all that appetizing; the grain was still white juice. Mom had me cut the unripe heads from the stalks and then make pincers out of the stalks. Then we used the pincers to strip the grain from the heads. Next we steamed the grain. After that we set the steamed grain out on mats to dry in the sun. It was dry by four o'clock that afternoon. Once it was dry, we pounded it to separate the chaff. The first steaming had solidified the white juice, and we could then steam it again for dinner. This was how we could eat unripe grain, by steaming it twice.

Once the harvest was in, we would celebrate. The whole town would take on a carnival atmosphere. It was then that the monotonous white everybody wore would give way to color, and traditional dancing would celebrate our heritage.

New years was double fun. We would celebrate the traditional new year on January first, then a month later we would celebrate the Buddhist new year. The latter, being tied to the lunar cycle was the more significant to our farming culture. It was the lunar calendar that told the farmers when to plant in the spring.

The lunar new year, being in mid winter, was observed with many indoor activities, such as the traditional Korean game of Yut. Yut, or Yut Nori is a board game that parents and children have played throughout the new year time for more than 1500 years. It is no more difficult than the Indian game of Parcheesi, though quite different in the way it is played. Plays are determined by casting four half-round sticks just as American gamers might throw dice. The rattle of the Yut sticks, punctuated by the cheers of the players, is as much a holiday sound to Korean children as the sound of sleigh bells is to Americans.

Only this picture, damaged in the war, remains of my early childhood. My teacher, Mr. Kioshi, is in the front row where the picture is torn. I am standing two rows behind him.

Chapter 2

How We Learned and Played

Education has always been highly valued in Korea, though when I was a boy, only about one in five were fortunate enough to get it, and even then it was difficult unless your family was wealthy. In that regard I was most fortunate. Although we were anything but wealthy, my mother often told me that learning was essential for survival, and insisted that I put learning in the highest priority. She cut corners and saved to meet the school costs. One way or the other, she was determined to see that I was schooled.

When I was seven or eight years old, she took me to the Korean schoolmaster's house to begin my schooling. This was a private school; the public schools were taught by Japanese teachers. The schoolmaster was an elderly gentleman, tall and thin, with a small, white beard. He was dressed all in white, the dress style of Korean adults in those days. He took down my name and told my mother what supplies to get. A few days later I proudly marched off to begin my first day at school.

I was directed to a large room in the schoolmaster's house. The class of ten or so were seated on the floor by low, square tables, one for each pupil. We used bamboo-handled brushes made of animal hair, and our ink was made of finely-ground pigment dissolved in water. The teacher would explain the meaning of a Chinese Hanja character, and we would practice at writing it down. In this way, we began to learn, one character at a time, the Hanja writing. While Korea does have a phonetic alphabet, many people still used Hanja in those days.

My first school book was titled, "Chen Ja Mun," which means, "One Thousand Words." Once we mastered that, we went on to another book in which the words were assembled into simple, four-word sentences such as, "The sky is blue," or "The earth is brown." After a couple hours of lessons, there was a morning recess, more lessons, and then we went home for lunch, to return by 2:00 in the afternoon.

Our teacher was a strict disciplinarian. He kept a bamboo switch on his table, and students who misbehaved, were late coming to class, or failed to do the assigned lesson were punished with a light stroke or two on the lower part of their legs.

After school we would go outside where we would play, catch fish, or hunt grasshoppers (a delicacy in Korea) which we would give to the teacher. We children played a variety of games. There was one called Hinada Boko, a Japanese term which means, "Sunshine Game." A small portion of a wall, most often facing south, would be blackened. This absorbed the sun's heat and it got very warm. One boy would stand against the blackened part enjoying its warmth while others would try to push him away and take over the warm place. If the blackened part of the wall was large enough, several boys would enjoy the warmth while a team would try to displace them. It was a rollicking, rough and tumble game.

Another game was similar to the American game of Hacky Sack. It was called Jagi Chagi. This was played by an individual, using a chagi, a device similar in appearance to a badminton shuttlecock. The player would stand on one foot and strike the shuttlecock with the inner side of the other foot. The object was to see how many times you could hit the chagi without having it touch the ground.

Horse Ride was played by two teams of five or six boys each. One team would form a line, each boy bent over with his head between the knees of the one in front, the first boy bracing his hands on any convenient, solid object. The other team would attempt to vault, one at a time onto the backs of the first team. The first one had the hardest vault. He had to land, if possible, on the back of the first "horse." The second had to make it onto the back of the boy immediately behind the first, and so on.

The girls played a game in which a rectangle, divided into eight blocks, was drawn on the ground. The player stood at a position at the end of the rectangle and tossed a small stone toward one square at a time. The object was to land the stone inside each square in turn, without having it touch a line.

One sport that was a lot of fun for the girls used a plank set up as a low teeter-totter. A girl would stand on one end while another jumped onto the other end, catapulting the first a few feet into the air.

Starting school not only awakened my desire to learn, it stirred the spiritual side of me as well. There was a Christian missionary school in P'unggi, about ten minutes walk from home. Every Sunday I would hear the bell calling the people to worship. It was a massive bell, and I would watch in fascination as its ponderous tongue swung back and forth. It seemed to be saying, "Chong ... dong ...chong ... dong." Chong dong is the Korean word for Heaven.

About the time I began schooling, I began to wonder about the Christians. Perhaps it was because the Korean schoolmaster had taught me more than just the Hanja writing, he had also taught me to think.

I would think about my brother, who used to go once a year to a temple in the mountains with a food offering. He would spend three days there, then come back, but I couldn't see how he benefited from that. He still had his drinking problem and often got into trouble. Then there was my mother. She would frequently recite prayers in the Buddhist manner, but it seemed to me that she didn't know the meaning or the purpose of the prayers. I felt that there had to be something more to worship than that, so I decided to check the Christians out.

My going to the Christian school was not a problem to the rest of my family, as Buddhism is very tolerant of other faiths. As for me, it was a positive and rewarding experience. We were divided into small classes, with a teacher for each class who would explain various aspects of the religion to us. The worship service took place after church school. We would sing hymns, have some prayers, and then the pastor would present a sermon. I began to learn what the prayers meant, to whom they were addressed, and why. I learned the Christian moral values concerning right and wrong – always to do what is right because it is right, and to avoid that which is wrong because it is wrong. Over the next few years I began to understand more and more about Christianity, and by the time I was ten, I began to see myself as a Christian.

Until 1945, our land was ruled by the Japanese, and they were trying to teach us their culture as a replacement for the Korean ways. They also began using our land as a staging ground for their wars, first with China, then with America in World War II. Their rule became more and more repressive. Men were sometimes taken from the towns to work in the mines and munitions factories in Japan; young women were occasionally taken away to service the soldiers in the Japanese military. One of my sisters avoided that by marrying a farmer in the nearby village of Sun-Hung. The Myen Chang and the administrative people under him, being Korean, were always under scrutiny of the police. Japanese police were everywhere, and we were all afraid of them.

On the other hand, the Japanese teachers in the public schools were nice to us children. I entered the public school when I was nine. We were required to learn Japanese, since the teaching of Korean in public schools was not allowed. We were even given Japanese names. My name was Na-ga-tani-shi-ro. The Korean language was forbidden to be spoken in the school.

The first grade was taught by a Korean woman under Japanese direction; the second grade teacher was a Japanese woman. My third-grade teacher was a Japanese man named Arimura Kioshi. He was very patriotic to his homeland. Each day before the start of classes, he would tell us all about Japan, and the reasons for being at war with America. Looking back at it now, I can only guess that many of those propaganda lectures were dictated by authorities higher up in the education system.

All the school children were encouraged to bring in waste paper and empty cans to be recycled for the war effort. The children in the higher grades would spend some time working in rice paddies or in vegetable gardens. At harvest time they helped with threshing and grinding the grain. This, we were told, was the way in which we helped with the war effort.

We were also taught military drill, marching to the sound of a band, and we practiced bayoneting effigies of Roosevelt and Chiang Kai Shek – Japan's enemies. They treated us as though Korea was a state or province of the Japanese nation. The only problem with that was that the Korean people didn't accept it.

I got along well with Mr. Kioshi because I was attentive and learned well. I have always had a fascination for other languages, and quickly became fluent in Japanese. One day after school he called to me. "I'm going fishing tomorrow," he said. "Would you like to come along?"

I had never been fishing before that. "Oh, really? May I?" I answered excitedly. Before he could reply, I ran home and asked my parents. They consented, and the following morning my teacher and I set out.

We followed the stream a short way until we found a quiet spot. Our fishing tackle consisted of a bag-like net held between two rods. Mr. Kioshi showed me how to hold the net in the water while he went a little way up stream and drove the fish toward me and into the net. I lifted the net out of the water, then jumped back as the fish began flopping about furiously. Mr. Kioshi laughed heartily as I timidly tried to pick them up, encouraging me even through his laughter. He showed me how to pick them up without being cut by the dorsal spines, and how to string the catch through the gills with willow shoots.

We fished most of the afternoon. Then we took the catch to his house where he showed me how to clean and grill them. I was amazed at how delicious they were. Freshly-caught fish have the best flavor if they are cooked immediately.

After that we had many pleasant fishing trips together, and we bonded well, quickly becoming good friends. After six years of elementary school, I graduated with the top grade in my class. I had taken the first steps along my road, but it was soon to take an unexpected, very unpleasant turn.

Chapter 3

The First Curve in the Road

My father and I were very close. He was a hard-working man, devoted to his family. He would often take me with him as he went into the hills to hunt for firewood. It was a long trek, seven to ten miles. All he had in the way of shoes were sandals made of rice straw, and the bottoms of his feet would often become cracked and bleeding. The only medication available for that was a salve made from rice.

He had to be careful to take only dead wood. The Japanese rulers had strict conservation laws concerning this, and the police would often check to be sure no green wood had been cut. One could go to jail for cutting green wood.

From the time I was very small, I would follow him to the fields where he taught me the skills of farming. We spent a lot of good time together. He would sit with me and tell me stories before I went to bed, and we would enjoy the holidays together. There were so many special, happy times.

In the winter time he would carry me in a sling on his back, to a neighbor's house where he and other men would sit, play cards, and smoke their long, bamboo pipes. The loser in the game would pay for the snacks. That house had no windows, and with the door closed against the winter cold, the smoke got very thick. Once it got so thick that I passed out. My father carried me home where I finally woke up. I was between six and seven at the time.

When I was twelve, my father attended a neighbor's funeral. After the burial, there was a reception, and food was served. When we got home, my father complained of feeling cold. He went to bed, and wouldn't accept any food. By the next day he was seriously ill. My mother went to a local pharmacist and tried to help my father with herbal cures, but they didn't work. The following day she went to the Mudang, a shaman, hoping to exorcise whatever was making him sick. There was a medical doctor in town, but most of the people preferred to go to the Mudang.

The Mudang performed an elaborate ceremony of singing, shouting, dancing and waving a sword about. It was no help. My father died a day or two afterward. I was in great distress over this, and I cried for a long time. Something inside told me that my mother would have better spent her money by taking my father to the medical doctor or to the hospital.

After my father died, the pleasant, idyllic life of my childhood ended. My family had little money to pay for me to go on to middle school, but my mother saw to it that I kept up with my studies, even when I was not in school. I would go to school, or help with my brother's work during the day, and study in the evening. Schooling gradually became harder and harder to obtain. I had to do whatever kind of work was available just to help my family survive. My younger brother was sent to live and work in the home of the local baker. There he was treated almost as though he were a slave.

Customarily the eldest son was responsible for caring for his parents in their old age. After my father died, my oldest brother moved to Samchuck, hoping to earn more money. He tried to start a business there and for a while he frequently sent money home to our mother. However, after a couple of years his business failed. He died shortly afterward, and his children ended up in my mother's care. They were sent to work as domestic helpers for another family who treated them very well.

The third eldest of my brothers had left home during World War II to avoid being drafted into the Japanese army. He moved north to Manchuria, and it was to be many years before I would see him again. His leaving had a profound effect on my mother. She kept a picture of him in a prominent place in our home. She would often look at the picture and cry. Every day she placed a food offering in front of it and recited a few Buddhist prayers, hoping that this would cause him one day to come home.

He almost made it home right after the world war ended. He had saved up enough money for a trip back to P'unggi, and with the end of Japanese occupation of Korea, he set out for home. He got as far as the Yalu River when he fell in with some bad company. They talked him into gambling away all his money. Bitterly ashamed of himself, he felt he had no choice but to go back to his home in Manchuria. He was to get no second chance for a long time. North Korea closed its borders shortly thereafter.

Another brother, the second eldest in the family, took over supporting the household after my father's death. He was a big fellow, and very strong, able to carry as heavy a load as two ordinary men. Because of his size and strength, there was always plenty of demand for his services, and he seldom had any trouble finding work. He was a hard worker, devoted to his family, but he also had his weaknesses. He had a drinking problem and wasted a lot of what he earned on that. He would often get drunk at night. Then he would get into fights, and sometimes even got into trouble with the police. He sold our house and the farmland. We had to leave the home I had known all my life and move into a rented house.

We saw little of the money my brother got from selling our home; he spent most of it drinking and gambling. As time went by the stress of supporting our family began to take its toll. There were times when he became downright abusive. He would become loud and argumentative toward my mother. Sometimes he even beat her. On occasions such as that, I could tell that he felt very badly about it the next day, but he never apologized.

One sore point that caused many of these arguments was the fact that I was studying while he was working. He kept saying that I should be working too, helping to bring in more income rather than keeping my nose buried in a book. He would get into arguments with my mother over it, and once he even turned on me, striking me hard on the head. I thought it was my fault, and after that I put my books aside and applied most of my efforts working. I would follow my brother as he went out to work in the fields and help him there as he worked. Sometimes he would put me to work in the fields with him; at other times he would send me to work in somebody else's field or house. Between the two of us we managed to earn enough money to get by.

I graduated elementary school when I was fifteen. My grades were the highest in my class, a fact that quickly got around town. Having graduated at the top of my class, I had an attack of vanity. These were hard times for my family and my help was needed to bring in more income. But I felt so ashamed of doing menial work in the fields that, when I followed my brother out to work, I kept my head covered with a cloth. I didn't want people to see the school's top student going out to do common labor in the rice paddies.

Chapter 4

The Americans Come

It was August of 1945. I was fourteen. I woke up one morning to news that the Japanese were gone. Somebody said that America had been victorious in the war. At first I didn't believe it. I hurried over to Mr. Kioshi's house, but my teacher was nowhere to be found. His house was empty and silent. He had left town very quietly the night before, disappearing forever from my life.

I hung around the crossroads for a while, listening for any more news. Everybody was talking about it. Rumors were everywhere. We had been under Japanese domination for so long a time that it was hard to believe they were gone for good. One rumor suggested that the Japanese had left only long enough to regroup and then they would be back to dominate us again and continue their war.

31

The Japanese police and their informers were gone. A lot of the townspeople bore grudges against the police, most of whom, being afraid of retribution, had fled for their lives. Any who stayed behind and were caught were severely beaten or killed. It was a time of great turmoil. In the first few weeks after the war ended, the people vented their rage over the many years of Japanese occupation and oppression, trashing the former homes of their oppressors and arresting Koreans that were known to have been informers or collaborators. However, Mr Kioshi's home wasn't touched, as he had been good to the children and had earned the respect of their parents.

With no police force of any kind, there was widespread looting of the shops and the homes of the wealthy. Trains from the north on the way to Pusan in the south stopped at P'unggi to take on water. When they did, bands of young men boarded and searched them, checking all the passengers, confiscating any weapons they had, and detaining any Japanese sympathizers or collaborators they could recognize. Those whom they detained were brutally beaten, sometimes even killed. The turmoil would continue for a few years until the new Korean government was established and functioning, and law enforcement personnel could be recruited and trained, but then it would get even worse.

All through my schooling, the Japanese teachers had told us that the Americans were monsters – enormous in size and barbaric in their behavior. Some of the children had even been told that the Americans would eat them. Other rumors said they would make slaves of us. Our elders cautioned us not to believe everything the Japanese had said, but we should nonetheless be careful of the Americans. They were, after all, foreigners, and their ways were not the same as our ways. Everybody was afraid.

Finally it happened. An American motorcade entered P'unggi, and I saw Americans for the very first time. Yes, they were larger in size than our people, but they were not really giants. The vehicles stopped and several GI's got out. They spoke a language I didn't know. One of them approached me. I began to back away, but curiosity eventually overcame fear. As he drew nearer, he held something out to me, as though he wanted me to take it. I held back. He broke off a little bit and ate it, still offering the rest to me. I swallowed hard, then I took it. Once I tasted it, I felt a bit foolish. It was candy. I told the younger children this and they all gathered around the GI's. That was the way the Americans convinced us that they meant us no harm – by first befriending the children. The children quickly caught on to the idea, and before very long, any American vehicle that appeared in P'unggi was followed by a swarm of children. The GI's obliged them generously, throwing gum and candy to them. They also gave food to the adults, sometimes even from their own rations.

That was the way the Americans convinced us that they meant us no harm – by first befriending the children. (Army Historical Foundation)

We soon began to see visits by the Americans as a positive thing, but for a long time we remained careful not to trust them too far. We slowly became less afraid of them and, for a while, the road ahead seemed a little easier, but our contact with the Americans was limited. They spent most of their time in the cities, and visits to rural towns like P'unggi were rare and short-lived.

My knowledge of Japanese served me well at this time. I could not yet understand the language of the GI's, but some of them knew a little Japanese so I was able to talk to them. While I didn't realize it at the time, this was an important milestone along my road.

I managed to get back into middle school in 1947. My mother had saved up about $500 for school costs. Schooling continued until the school closed in 1950, with the start of hostilities between North and South Korea.

The American GI's had radios in their vehicles, which were always turned on, and sometime during that period (1945 to 1950) I first heard English spoken, and heard American music on the radios. The sounds of spoken English fascinated me, and I resolved to learn the language. This was where the Japanese I had learned from Mr. Kioshi came in handy. I bought a large Japanese-English dictionary, which not only gave the English translation of Japanese words that I already knew, but also the pronunciation of the English words, and I began, a word at a time, and with some help from the GI's, to learn English. It was the start of a long, slow process that would some day serve me well on the road ahead.

At that time, I was unaware of the extent to which the super powers had been bickering among themselves over the destiny of our country. At the Potsdam Conference in 1945, the Unites States and Russia could not reach an agreement on a unified Korea. The United States wanted to set up a democratic government; Russia insisted on a communist government. Neither side would give an inch, so Korea was divided between Russia and the United States at the 38th parallel. This was not the first time that particular boundary had been used; it had been set up between Japan and Russia as early as 1900. Then it vanished in 1910 when Japan won their war with Russia, only to come back and haunt us now.

It was during the same time period that homes in P'unggi got their first electric lighting, instantly driving the dim, smelly oil lamps into the past. Life was now changing at an ever-increasing pace. Korea would never again be the special kind of country it once was. Enormous changes were about to take place in the lives of all our people, changes that would uproot families and utterly destroy most of the lifestyle we had known. One might argue that, once the changes were made and we were settled into the new ways, life would be better, but the changes would nonetheless be painful for all of us. There were to be many more unexpected curves on the road ahead, and some of them would be most unpleasant.

Chapter 5

The Road Becomes Rough

I didn't know it at the time, but my road was about to become very rough indeed. Our nation's government was very young, as governments go, and its people still had a long way to go in learning how to govern themselves. Various political groups competed, sometimes violently, to establish their places in the political structure, while communists from the north infiltrated the south, adding to the already confused political mess.

The South Korean government was established in 1948, and the North Korean government shortly thereafter. Until then there was no government at all except for local people's committees. In 1945 the people's committees had tried to unite into a central government, but the United States refused to recognize it. Neither did the United States recognize the exiled Korean Provisional

39

Government led by Sygnman Rhee. Until some kind of government could be set up, the whole country languished in a state of absolute political chaos, and at the civilian level, it sometimes got downright ugly.

I had a cousin who was a member of the Korean Young Men's Association, a guerrilla organization supporting Sygnman Rhee's political views. They published a newspaper, and my cousin put me to work making collections from its subscribers. I had many opportunities to observe what the Young Men's Association did. They were often the only defense the townspeople had against roving bands of troublemakers that came down from the north burning, vandalizing, and sabotaging. They also hunted down communist sympathizers and took them into custody, at which time they were often tortured and killed. Such things were done by both sides. I was in my late teens at the time, still too young to take part, but I saw some of these incidents myself.

It was a frightening thing to see. The communist troublemakers hid out in the hills during the day, but one cannot stay awake forever.

They would eventually come home and go to bed. Then the Young Men's Association would strike, descending upon the home of a known troublemaker around three in the morning. He would be taken to the Association headquarters and there brutally interrogated. From there, if he were determined to deserve such a fate, he would be taken out of town beneath a bridge and shot. Terrible as it sounds, with no government protection yet available to the townspeople, the Young Men's Association felt that there was no alternative but to take matters into their own hands. It was a tragic, brutal time.

I recall one fellow who lived up in the hills outside of town. He was both a pharmacist and a doctor. He knew all the available medicinal plants, where to find them and how to process them. He was a highly-respected member of the community, well-liked and prosperous. His sympathies were democratic, but those of his two sons were communist. He frequently came to the Young Men's Association headquarters and gave them large donations, at the same time begging them to be lenient with his sons, should they be taken. I recall seeing the extreme sadness in his face as he left the association headquarters; he was sick with worry over his sons. So far as I know, the sons were never caught, but if they had been, leniency would not have been given.

During the years when the Young Men's Association was most active, North Korea became more and more belligerent toward the south, and soon was voicing a claim to all of Korea. Tensions between the two escalated at an alarming rate, and South Korea was at a disadvantage, both economically and militarily. The North Korean army were experienced, battle-hardened soldiers, well-trained by the Russians, and combat ready. The South Korean army was not only poorly trained and equipped, it had been significantly weakened by a communist-led revolt in 1948, and by the purge that followed.

After the end of World War II, the American policy had been aimed toward setting up a peaceable government, rather than preparing for another war. Most of the U.S. forces were withdrawn in 1949, leaving just a handful of military advisers in South Korea. These military advisers were not combat experienced, and the

U.S. was directing most of its attention to the iron curtain in Europe, leaving Korea on the back burner. Looking back now at this oversight, it takes on the appearance of having been a tremendous political and military blunder.

The North Koreans openly invaded the south on June 25, 1950. My whole family was very frightened when we learned of this. Because of my cousin's involvement in the Young Men's Association, if we were caught by communist forces, it would mean certain death, and possibly torture for all of us. There was little we could do but watch and wait as the battle lines drew ever closer, and hope that the enemy would be stopped before they got to P'unggi.

In just a few days the inevitable happened. I was out by the stream west of town when I suddenly heard a lot of gunfire to the north. I knew that the war was upon us, just hours away, maybe less. I ran home to tell my family, but there was little need of that; they had heard it too. Then we heard more gunfire — two or three shots close by.

Fear took over. I grabbed a blanket, some cooking utensils, a kettle, a spoon and some food, and put them into a backpack. My elder brother got some more blankets and food; my mother carried some extra clothing in a bundle on her head. Then we set out as fast as we could go. Now we were refugees, and there were many more like us, all heading south, a growing stream of humanity fleeing the fighting. We were all together in the same predicament – a refugee tribe.

A mile or so down the road I met a friend's sister, who was an elementary school teacher. She was heading back to her home to look after her family. Her face was filled with fear and worry. I never heard how she made out, but I did hear that her family managed to hide from the communists until they left.

We walked another two miles or so, then we rested by the river. There was a lot of gravel there, not too comfortable to sit down upon. Otherwise, it was a beautiful, shady spot – very peaceful and calm, so far removed from the terror we had just fled. We washed up and chatted with some of our road companions, sharing our experiences and fears, while the children played in the stream.

Thank God for the little children! Those whom we would consider the weakest and most vulnerable were also the strongest in some ways. Even in this time of misery and fear they could still play, and they were often the only source of much-needed laughter.

A vast river of humanity fleeing the fighting.
(From U.S. Army Historic Collection Online.)

We continued on several more miles, then stopped for the night. Our sleep was shallow; the ground is seldom a comfortable bed. Several of us chatted for a while, wondering if the enemy could be pushed back so that we could go home, but that was not to be. In the morning we again heard artillery explosions to the north, and we all scrambled to get on our way again. Now, however there were more of us. In this way we pressed onward, day after day, part of an ever-growing river of humanity, each day hoping the next would find us homeward bound, and each day having our hopes shattered by the continued approach of war.

When misfortune uproots a great number of people, be it war or some other calamity, it reveals both the best and the worst of human nature. Such was our situation. It was a time that is still painful in my memory. At the same time many of us were reaching out to one another, strangers comforting strangers, and sharing each other's misery, we also had to watch out lest what little we had be stolen. There was one family carrying their belongings in an ox-drawn cart. Their ox was stolen and butchered for its meat.

Children would sometimes become separated from their parents. The lucky ones were found again. Others would wind up being adopted by persons who had lost their own children. Some would simply die by the roadside. Everywhere there was grief and misery.

We continued on day after day with the tens of thousands of other refugees, a large, flowing river of humanity, helping one another whenever we could, sometimes even putting blankets over our sleeping neighbors. Those who had the skill made frameworks to support tents. Each day we traveled ten miles or so, then camped for the night, sleeping on the ground. The war seemed to be chasing us – we frequently heard distant explosions and sometimes the rattle of small arms fire.

The nights were warm, which was a good thing. On the other hand, we were all but eaten alive by the mosquitoes. People who hadn't wanted to be refugees stayed home and greeted or hid from the communist forces, who killed any whom they could find.

My role was to beg for food from homes we passed on the way – house to house, town to town. I will never forget the generosity of the many strangers who gave freely of what little they had. Without their kindness, we would all have died of hunger.

We were favored with fair weather for the first two weeks, then the rain came. When it came, it came with a vengeance – thunder and lightning, and strong wind. We set up makeshift shelters with blankets spread over branches. Some of us huddled against nearby houses, taking shelter under the eves. Often the occupants invited us in. Many houses were empty, their owners having fled, and we took shelter in them. Those who couldn't find shelter were miserable, soggy, wretched creatures.

We followed the river south to Andong, then to Yongchon. From there we turned west until, three weeks after we had left home, we arrived at Taegu, about a hundred miles from Pusan, where many refugees were settling into a large encampment. There we stayed as Korean and American forces battled to defend the Pusan perimeter. I felt that I was needed to help defend my country rather than wait out the war in a refugee camp. I volunteered for the Korean Army, much to my mother's distress. I'll never forget our parting – how we hugged and cried together, neither of us knowing whether we would ever see each other again.

Chapter 6

The War Gets Personal

Basic training was short, very short, just two weeks. Our country was backed into a corner, fighting for its very life, and needed to get men into the field as quickly as possible. After basic training, I found myself in a recruitment holding area where we waited while the military authorities checked our backgrounds. Once our backgrounds were verified, the different units of the military selected such men as they needed.

I was there two weeks. Finally, an American, dressed in civilian clothing arrived. He selected twenty men, including me. We were put onto a bus and taken to a private house. There we had lunch, and then each of us was interviewed through an interpreter. When my turn came up, I was totally unprepared for what he had to say. "Your mission," he said, "will be to enter the enemy territory and play the role of a refugee. As you make your way back, you are to find out what you can about the enemy – how many there are, what kinds and how many weapons they have." In other words, I would be a spy – a far more personal involvement in the war than if I were a soldier. This was at once fascinating and frightening. In the game of war, spying is both the most elite and the most dangerous kind of play.

Once we had been briefed as to our function, the American selected a few of our number and left with them. Over the next few days he would return daily, select two or three more, and leave. Eventually I was the only one left. When he came back for me, he took me in his car to an outpost at Ankong, near the city of Yongchon, where fighting was in progress. It was a very large battle, with much gunfire, rockets, and artillery. I later learned that it was part of a major turning point in the war, as U.N. and South Korean troops struggled to defend the Pusan perimeter. I was kept there overnight under the supervision of a Korean Army sergeant, who was in charge of intelligence. Needless to say, I slept little that night with the sounds of the battle raging all around me. By morning, the battle was over, and the sergeant took me with him around the battlefield. Abandoned weapons, dead and dying men and horses were everywhere. It was a sickening, frightening sight. Our side had won a great victory, but it was an expensive one. Afterward, the sergeant questioned me in detail on what I had seen.

Later that day, my American boss came by and received the sergeant's report of my performance. We then got into his car and headed north in search of the enemy, but none were to be seen. Then he took me east to the coast where I was put on board a fishing boat. I was told that I would be dropped off up north, and I was to make my way back by road, as a refugee, looking out for enemy presence – how many there were and what weapons they had.

The boat carried me north about 30 miles or so, and then I was put ashore. I had no military identification, I carried no weapons and I wore no uniform. I had the basic equipment for my sustenance that refugees usually carried, and a little food. To make my situation more believable, I was supposed to beg for some of my food. In this condition I made my way back by road, as just another of the many refugees. I chatted with other refugees, being careful not to let on my real purpose or how I came to be there, listening for any mention of the enemy, and always looking out for them. I saw no sign of them. They had apparently been driven far to the north.

As I made my way south, the awful price that civilians pay for the war was to be seen everywhere. Every town was in a state of ruin. Everybody was homeless; everybody was a refugee. Their only comfort was knowing that the enemy had been driven away.

I made it back to the Yongchon area in a couple of days. There I reconnected with my boss and reported on my experiences as thoroughly as I could. Having seen or heard nothing of the enemy, I felt almost as though my mission had been useless. My boss didn't share this feeling; he was pleased with my report. He said that I had done very well. Then he began talking about a new mission.

The following day we got into his car and set out into the mountains. My boss knew exactly where he was going, as we made our way over deserted back roads around the ends of the front lines, and deep into enemy territory. We drove to Chongjin, a city in the extreme northern part of the country. This was a two-day trip, and we stopped overnight at an inn. There we had a chance to chat informally with one another. I told him my story, and when I mentioned that I was a Christian, he seemed to take special interest. "I'm a Christian too," he said, and we chatted for a while about being Christians before turning in for the night.

The following day we arrived at Chongjin. We then drove inland to a place called Mu Ju Ku Chon Dong. Finally my new mission was explained to me. From Mu Ju Ku Chon Dong I was to travel and observe as I had done before, while making my way back to Chongjin.

This posed a problem. I was from the south, and we were now in the extreme north of the country. While the language there was essentially the same, there were significant differences in accent and dialect, just as there are between the extreme north and south in the United States. Should I be stopped and questioned by the locals, the first few words out of my mouth to anybody would instantly betray my origin, and I would almost surely be taken, tortured and killed, just as were the communist sympathizers at the hands of the Korean Young Men's Association in the south. I told my boss that, unless I had a weapon with which to defend myself, I wouldn't go.

What happened next was perhaps the most frightening moment of my entire life. My boss ordered me to stand in the roadway. Then he walked off a little way, turned and aimed his pistol at me. My heart sank. I was about to be killed on this deserted road far from my home. My body would lie there in the dust like a dead dog. Nobody would know who I was or how I came to be there. My family would never know what had become of me. I just stood there, expecting any moment to feel the bullet crashing through my body, but he didn't fire. Apparently he could not find it in his heart to kill me. Why, I don't know. I'll probably never know. Perhaps it was because he had said the day before that he was a Christian, and he knew that I too was a Christian. I just don't know.

I felt sick inside – angry and frustrated by this turn of events. Death had been, for that brief moment, staring into my face. I had done no wrong, just tried to exercise a little common sense. After what seemed to be an eternity, my boss put his pistol away. "All right," he said at last, "get back in the car." He was silent as we drove south, back into friendly territory. At Hwangam, he put me on board an American LST. He paid me well the services I had performed and provided some paperwork instructing the U.S. forces as to my status. Then he shook my hand and wished me well. That was the last I ever saw of him.

(Naval Historical Foundation)

The LST was an amazing craft, especially to me, a country boy. I had never seen so large a ship before, much less been on board one. The very sight of it at Hwangam, with its massive bow doors wide open, boggled my mind. It carried me south to Pusan, a two-day trip.

From Pusan I was put onto a train which took me north to Wonjo where I was reconnected with the ROK army. I stayed there a couple of weeks with a Korean sergeant, who listened to an account of my experiences. He then offered me a choice, either to join his unit or to go with the American forces. I chose to serve with the U.S. forces. I felt this would be a chance for me to continue learning English, and that life in general would be easier. This was fine with the sergeant. He provided me with suitable credentials so that I could go to the U.S. encampment and apply for work there.

I presented my credentials at the U.S. base and soon found myself working as a house boy under the supervision of a civilian who did administrative work. At first it seemed to be an agreeable situation. I cared for his quarters, did his laundry, and whatever other chores he would have me do. We got along well, and I began to feel safe. This went on for several weeks. Then, once more, my road took an unexpected turn for the worse.

Telling what happened here is perhaps the most difficult of this entire account. I was going about my work as usual when my employer called to me and demanded that I gratify his sexual wants in a most vile and disgusting way. "You suck a hojie," he said.

"What!?" I could hardly believe what I heard. What manner of a creature did he think I was? I am not an animal; I'm a human being – a Christian. I refused.

He opened his trousers and dropped his undershorts, exposing his enormous, ugly private part, then repeated his demand. I shook my head and backed away. He became angry and more insistent. "You suck a hojie," he said again.

Some time long before this I had been taught that one should stand up for that which is clearly right, no matter what the consequences. "No. I don't do that," I emphasized.

My employer would not accept this. He pointed to his exposed part and swore at me. "You suck a hojie. That's an order," he yelled. I stood my ground, and the consequence was quick and heavy. He glared at me, consumed with anger and hatred. "All right, I'll fix you, you little gook," he growled. "Get your things and get in the car."

I did as he said, all the time believing he was only going to fire me. I would soon be rid of him and working for a new and nicer boss, but he had other things in mind. While I was waiting for him, he altered my records to indicate that my status was that of a prisoner of war, rather than soldier or refugee. Taking my papers with him, he got into the car without saying another word. He didn't even look at me.

The car drove up to the main gate of the POW compound, where my adversary spoke briefly with the guard. The gates were opened, the car went in, and the gates swung shut behind me. Now I realized what he was up to. Now I was really scared. I was told to get out of the car and take my belongings with me. A stern-faced GI motioned me toward a tent.

"What's going on?" I protested. "I'm not a prisoner. I'm a South Korean soldier." But nobody listened. I was searched, and my clothes exchanged for POW clothing. It was a couple of days before I was interviewed, and by then I was afraid to tell what had really happened, lest he should try to get even with me for informing on him. Then I could be brought to even greater harm.

It is difficult to describe all my feelings at this point. What had I done to deserve this? I had started out with an earnest desire to serve my country. Now, suddenly, I was a prisoner of my own people, presumed an enemy. Nobody would listen to me, and even if they did, nobody would believe me. Never before in my whole life had I felt so alone, so confused, or so frightened.

Chapter 7

I Sit Out the War

When I arrived at the POW compound, I was first housed in a receiving tent for incoming POW's, along with a couple dozen or so others. There I was issued my prisoner clothing, and a few days later I was transferred to a POW camp on Koje Island, off the coast near Pusan. There I was to remain for the duration of the war. When I was assigned to what was to be my quarters, I found my fellow prisoners to be mostly anti communist. This was both a great surprise and a relief. There were South Korean civilians who had stumbled across U.S. soldiers in the battle zones. There were ROK soldiers who had become separated from their units. All were to be considered POW's until their credentials could be verified – a thing that never happened, so far as I know.

The POW complex was a large, open area surrounded by high, barbed-wire fences, with

63

guard towers every fifty feet or so. Inside it was divided into about 40 camps, each camp consisting of 20 tents. POW's were housed 30 or so to a tent. In the winter the tents were heated by oil-burning stoves, two to a tent, and that was sufficient to keep us comfortable. There were faucets distributed about the camp for drinking water; water for washing was in a common wash tub between each pair of camps. Latrines were shared, each one common to two camps, and consisted of a dozen or so 50-gallon oil drums, cut in half, with wooden seats on top. Each day a detail from one of the tents would carry the drums, under guard, to a dumping area a mile or so removed from the camp.

Regardless whether or not we were prisoners, the Korean war went on inside the POW compound. The inmate population was divided into two factions, some camps for known communist sympathizers, and some for those who had said they were anti communist. This division was necessary to keep the two factions from killing each other off, but they tried to do so anyway.

PRISONERS LEARN TO WORK TIN IN THE KOJE-DO CAMP

I had kept my Japanese-American dictionary with me. I cut up an empty rations can to make a metal box in which to keep it.

PICTURE OF STALIN DISPLAYED DURING A POW DEMONSTRATION, KOJE-DO

The communist camps exercised such complete control over their own compounds that the U.N. guards dared not enter.

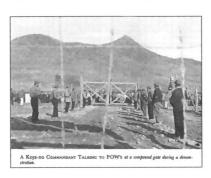

A KOJE-DO COMMANDANT TALKING TO POW's *at a compound gate during a demonstration.*

ONE OF THE NEW COMPOUNDS ON KOJE-DO, *showing the double rows of barbed wire surrounding each enclosure. An evacuated village in the background is being burned to prevent the exchange of information between prisoners and villagers.*

They fought with rocks and home made,
improvised weapons.
(From: http://www.kmike.com/TruceTent/ch11.htm
Represented by website owner as Public Domain)

With the landing at Inchon, and the turning of the tide of the war around Pusan, large numbers of POW's had been taken, and the United Nations forces were ill equipped to properly house and supervise them. The compounds on Koje Island had been set up in a hurry, and were quickly filled to as much as five times their capacity. Inmates vastly outnumbered the guards. The guards had been trained to be soldiers, not prison guards, and they could do little more than keep the prisoners contained. With a total inmate population exceeding 120,000, and the dangerously insufficient number of guard personnel, life within the camps was a tense and dangerous situation at its best. Each camp had its own internal structure and organized its own inmate guard force. The communist camps exercised such complete control over their own compounds that the U.N. guards dared not enter.

Inmates on each side had run tunnels to the other. The tunnels were used for raids, one side on the other. Inmates were frequently kidnapped by raiding parties from the opposite camp, and brought to the opposing side where they were beaten up. There even were a lot of murders. They fought with rocks and home made, improvised weapons. Tensions boiled over when the communist camp captured General Dodd, the prison commandant, and held him hostage for several days, holding their own "court," and trying him for imagined "crimes" until certain demands were met. I was unaware at the time what a potentially explosive situation it was, or how close it came to erupting into a massive blood bath.

One winter's day, I made a wrong turn on my way back from the latrine and found myself at the communist camp. I was immediately seized by a POW guard. "What are you doing here?" he demanded. Before I could answer, he accused me of coming over with the intent to steal. I was kicked and beaten unconscious. When I awoke, I was lying in the space between the two camps.

Following the incident with General Dodd, the whole POW complex was rebuilt. Individual camps were separated by as much as half a mile. Outside the prison area, a couple of whole villages were moved to prevent communist communication with the outside. With the communist camps a great distance away from the South Korean camps, life seemed a little safer, and conditions became more tolerable.

My POW life eventually settled into a routine. Each morning we would line up outside the tents where the guards would check to ensure that none had escaped. Then all the members of our camp would shout anti communist slogans and sing South Korean patriotic songs. At the same time the Communist camps would shout their slogans and sing Communist songs. It was a loud and noisy time.

We ate well. Food was purchased locally as well as imported in the form of military rations. We would line up at meal time to receive our rations, and after eating we would clean our utensils to get them ready for the next meal. Work details were limited to work necessary in maintaining the camp.

We had a tent set aside for Christian worship for those who so desired. Christian missionary clergy would come in and hold regular services there. After the services we were given counseling by the clergy, from which I received much reassurance and comfort. We also had an outdoor auditorium where we could stage plays and whatever other entertainment we wished.

For many of us, life in general was better than what we may have experienced outside the camp.

In a way, the evil that one man had wanted to do to me turned out to be a blessing in disguise. I was away from the battles, I had enough to eat, I was warm in winter time, and once the communist camp was moved away, I was comparatively safe. All that was wrong was that I wasn't free. Other than that, I can say that the man's effort to do me wrong had nicely backfired.

I wondered why we who were anti communist should remain prisoners when we could be of greater use helping to fight the war. It was generally believed that the U.S. policy wanted to keep its numbers of POW's high so that, when an exchange should be agreed upon, they could have a number equal to or greater than the number of prisoners held by North Korea. This was what we believed, although it was never verified. Whatever was the case, I had little choice but to sit out the war as a prisoner of my own people.

Except for the occasional work details, there is little a prisoner can do but wait. I kept myself occupied by keeping up my efforts to learn English. Most of my possessions had been lost; I had left them along with all my money in the care of a Korean woman living near my employer in Wonju, and I never saw them again. She probably wondered why I never came back to reclaim them. However, I had kept my Japanese-American dictionary with me. I cut up an empty rations can to make a metal box in which to keep it. Part of my motivation to keep studying English was the belief that, had I been more proficient in that language, I might have been able to present my case well enough to be set free.

Far away in Panmunjon, peace talks were begun, stopped, resumed, stopped, and started again with no apparent progress. We later learned that the sticking point was North Korea's embarrassment over the large number of POW's who didn't want to go back to the north. At one point, the South Korean government became tired of waiting, and ROK guards were instructed to allow many South Korean prisoners and anti communists to escape. Some 27,000 simply left the prison compounds and entered the civilian population. I was not that fortunate; my camp was too well guarded.

Time dragged on. Finally, in 1953, an armistice was signed. Prisoners were exchanged, with those not wishing to return to their former countries being detained for a period of time. The Neutral Nations Repatriation Commission was set up in the Demilitarized Zone, where 22,000 Chinese and North Korean prisoners, and 350 UN non-repatriates were housed. In the end, the Communists could only persuade 600 to come back to their side; the rest went to Taipei or to India.

Back at Koje Island, the long-awaited day finally came for me. We got our things together and were marched to a large tent. As we went in, we were given our choice: Those wanting to go back to the north stepped to one side of the tent; those preferring to remain with the south stepped to the other. Those of us choosing to remain in the south were put onto a boat and taken to the mainland. It was quite an emotional experience as the boat pulled away from the pier and I looked back for the last time at that island where I had lived for the previous couple of years. Once on the mainland, we were taken to a house where I cleaned up, and I washed away the grime of those years as a prisoner. In a few days we were provided with clean clothing and transportation home.

Our land had suffered greatly from the war.
(From U.S. Army Historic Collection Online.)

I cannot describe my feelings as I made my way back to P'unggi. My homeland had suffered so much, first from the Japanese occupation up to World War II, then from the invasion out of the north. Every town I passed through lay in ruin – homes had been destroyed and sacked. Much of the usable timber had been stripped from the forests. Everywhere there were whole families that had been uprooted and scattered. Some had been wiped out completely.

P'unggi lay in ruin. Only a few houses remained of a town that had once been home to over 6,000 people. I had no idea whether or not my mother had managed to get back, or even if she was still alive. I searched for days, hoping to find somebody that might know, and finally I met a distant relative who told me where I could find my mother. She was staying in a one-room shack, one of the few remaining houses.

It was an emotional reunion. As I approached the shack, my mother came running out, screaming with joy and relief. "Is it really you?" she cried, "Oh, son, I thought you were dead. I thought you were dead." We fell into each other's arms and cried together for a long time. Then my mother told me her own tale.

We had fled P'unggi as a family, my mother, myself, and my older brother. My younger brother had fled with the baker's family he had been working for. When I left them to join the army, my older brother also went his own way. The result was that my mother was left by herself with nobody to find food for her, and she nearly starved. During the most crucial part of the war, Taegu was nearly lost to the enemy. My mother had fled Taegu along with thousands of other refugees. She made her way on foot to a refugee camp in Miryang and wintered there. Then, with the fighting steadily moving to the north, she began making her way back to the P'unggi area as soon as spring set in.

It took much longer for my mother to get back to P'unggi than it had taken for us to get to Taegu. She was all by herself, with nobody to beg food for her. Without the generosity of many strangers and the GI's who willingly gave part of their own rations to refugees on the road, she would certainly have starved to death. As it were, she was on the road several months before finally reaching what was left of P'unggi. With nobody to document the odyssey, one can only imagine the suffering she endured along the way. It was a journey of well over one hundred miles, and once she got there, an even more tragic responsibility awaited.

My younger brother had not been treated very well by the baker's family with whom he had fled. They had returned to P'unggi long before my mother, and quickly resumed their business. To the bakers, my brother was almost a slave. In the bakery business, one has to be up very early so that the bread might be ready to eat by breakfast. My brother had to see to all the details of getting the fire going in the oven, fixing breakfast for the family, cleaning up, even doing the family's laundry. He was allowed little or no rest over a long working day. If he was lucky, he got five hours or so sleep at night. He came down with tuberculosis, and they sent him back to my mother, fearful that they might contract his illness.

My mother now had the task of caring for an exhausted, half-starved, dying son. Food was scarce in those times. Everybody was close to starving, and my mother, desperate to get some protein into her son, had even cooked up a very unfortunate cat and fed him the meat. Even that was not enough to help. There was little anybody could do for him in that war-torn country, and he soon died. He was buried outside of town, on the hillside.

My cousin and his associates in the Young Men's Association had gone underground and fought a guerrilla warfare against the invaders from the north. He was a local hero, greatly respected around P'unggi, but I was unable to get into touch with him. It was just as well. How could I explain to him why I had sat out the war in the

POW camp while others were fighting and dying on the battlefield? POW life had taken its toll on me. I felt bitterly embarrassed and ashamed, and I kept to myself as much as possible. I just didn't want to talk about where I'd been.

This was what I had come home to. It was a miserable time – no food, no jobs, and the whole country lay in ruin. Our farm was gone, sold long ago by my older brother. He had made his way back home, and was living with my mother. To his credit, he willingly did any kind of work he could find. His was the only income for the family, but his bad habits were still present. He often got into trouble. Still he was a hard worker. I went with him to help out in any way I could. We all were struggling hard just to survive. Then, as if things weren't bad enough, I got my draft notice scarcely two months later. Once again I had to part from my mother and leave her with all that uncertainty.

Chapter 8

Soldier to Officer

Being recalled into military service did have
its positive side. Now I had a second chance
to serve my country and to put aside the
stigma I felt over the POW episode. I reported for
duty at the recruitment center in P'unggi, and was
put on board a train to Pusan along with several
others. From there we were taken by boat to Jeju
Island for basic training. This time the training was
longer and more intense than it had been the first
time around. Then we had been at war and it had
been necessary to get men into the field as quickly
as possible. Now they had the time to make the
training more thorough. I couldn't send any
allotment home to my mother, however. The
Korean government had no funds to pay the
common soldiers – only the officers.

During basic training, I injured my knee. My
squad was involved in a field exercise with

weapons and full packs. We were charging up a hill, pausing to go into a crouch and fire, then rising to charge again. As I rose to continue the charge, something snapped inside my knee. My leg buckled beneath me, and down I went in pain, unable to get up. The squad leader urged me to try again. I tried, but it was no use. The pain was too much. The ambulance took me to the hospital, and I was there for a full month.

Once again, what had first seemed to be a setback turned out to be a lucky break. In the hospital, I had time to study and to make some plans. My knowledge of English, incomplete though it was, now served me in good stead. I put in an application for officer candidate training. The test was in English, and I passed it with a high score. Once out of the hospital, I had to repeat the basic training before I could begin officer candidate training, but as soon as basic training was finished, I was sent to the army infantry school at Kwangju for the officer candidate course. Again the English language served me well; many of the texts had come from the U.S. and were in English. After an advanced infantry course, I was sent on to Kumhae for engineering training. Finally, eighteen months after I had reported for duty, I was commissioned second lieutenant. Now I had a steady income. I could send money home to better my mother's life.

I was first assigned to 1107th Field Combat Corps Headquarters as platoon leader of a road maintenance unit. Not long after that, I was called out to head up a security guard platoon. Our duty was to guard the perimeter of the base, one squad at the main gate, one on the eastern perimeter, one on the west, and one in the hills to the north. Each morning we were all supposed to assemble at the headquarters by the main gate for briefing.

One morning the north squad didn't show up. I sent a detail out to check on them. When the detail didn't come back, I sent a second. Still no answer. Finally a third detail returned. Their report was rather disturbing: "They're all drunk and unconscious."

"What do you mean, drunk?" I asked incredulously. "There's no booze available out there."

"Just what I said. They're all drunk. I couldn't wake any of them up"

"You're sure they're alive?"

"Well, they are breathing."

"What could have they been drinking?"

"Don't know, but the place stinks of alcohol."

I sent a squad out to bring them in. They were all so drunk that the squad couldn't wake them up. Each one of them had to be carried back. It was quite a sight, a whole squad making their way back to headquarters, each one with the limp form of a man on his back.

I reported the situation higher up, and called for a medical dispatch. They were taken then to the hospital to sober up. Once they were awake, it took a lot of questioning both by myself and by the criminal investigation unit to finally get to the bottom of the situation. The men had helped themselves to a supply of anti freeze from the motor pool, and had a party. Now, the alcohol in anti freeze is different from that in booze, which means that these men were very lucky not to be dead or blind. A lot of investigation, written statements and digging by the Criminal Investigation Division finally determined that I had done no wrong, but still, as their commanding officer, I bore the ultimate responsibility. I was reassigned to the road maintenance unit.

When all is said and done, my new assignment proved to be far more agreeable than guard duty. I got a lot of satisfaction from rebuilding roads and bridges that had been torn up during the war. I was able to make good use of the skills I had learned in the engineering training. I was helping a land ravaged by war to heal, and with each project we completed, I felt that the place was a bit better for my having been there.

My outfit relocated to the Wonju area where we became an extension of a quartermaster unit with the job of expanding a storage warehouse. Then for the next two years I worked on a number of projects ranging from putting up new buildings to clearing away war debris and rebuilding structures that had been damaged during the war. We built barracks, mess halls, headquarters offices, utility structures, whatever was needed to rebuild the military infrastructure. It a satisfying, rewarding experience.

Our job was to build and maintain military facilities, but even the most hard-hearted soldier would find it difficult to be totally blind to the plight of the civilian sector and the squalor that the war had brought upon them. Wonju had been lost and retaken twice, and there was a great deal of rebuilding to be done. Our equipment and supplies were supposed to be for military use only. That's what the rules said, but there were times when the rules were bent and there were times when the rules were utterly ignored. There was no set procedure for allowing our equipment to be used in civilian projects. Still, wherever there was a need – whether it was filling in a pit dug by wartime artillery or leveling the ground for a schoolyard, and if a bulldozer was available, the job would get done.

It is common practice to order a little more material than is actually calculated to complete a project, a precaution against the unexpected. Material left over from a completed project on the base would usually find its way to some place, military or civilian, where it could do the most good.

Only a fool would believe that motives for such things were entirely altruistic. Certainly there was often a great deal of satisfaction in helping others, but that was not always the case. There were times when money did indeed change hands under the table. Ours was, after all, a very young government and corruption of one kind or another was present from the bottom to the very top. One certain person high up in the ranks was known to us as "The Big Fish." It was he who decided where equipment or materials would go, and sometimes it was for a price. When he was paid off, however, only a small portion of it went into his own pockets. There were expenses to seal the lips of his superiors; there were expenses to quiet the Criminal Investigation Division, and he took good care of the men serving under him. Surplus material often found its way to improve the interiors of their barracks, and to enhance their overall comfort. There were plenty of recreational activities for the men that would not have otherwise been possible.

There comes to mind one project I supervised, putting up a large building for the motor pool. The walls and roof of the building were to be covered with corrugated sheet metal. When the materials were requisitioned, there was the usual 10% over the calculated amount drawn. My commander took charge of the leftovers, and presently a new structure appeared on the base to shelter the furnace that heated our barracks in winter. As the motor-pool building neared completion, an officer higher up wanted to make a name for himself, so he pulled a surprise inspection. As he looked the building over he meticulously counted the corrugated sheets on the walls and roof of the 22,500 square foot structure. Then he came to me. "How many sheets of corrugated did you use?" he asked.

I told him 145, which was the amount that had been requisitioned.

"Bullshit!" he snapped, punctuating his reply with his combat boots against my shins. "I just counted, and there's only 130. Now what became of the other 15?"

What was I to do, rat on my immediate superior? I said, "I don't know"

"Bullshit!" he snapped again with another blow to my legs. "They're right over there in that hut, and you know it!"

I shrugged, and he stalked away, leaving me with two sore legs and a wounded ego. Of course he knew what went on. He had done much the same thing himself when he was buttering up his way to his present position. While it was technically my job to keep account of supplies, answering sticky questions such as this was better left to my commanding officer.

I took a 6-month instructor's course in Tae Kwon Do, graduating with a third degree green belt, and then I taught Martial Arts for a little over a year. While doing that I also took a course in Chemical Biological and Radiological Warfare and instructed in those subjects.

There was a certain sergeant major serving under me who had an attitude. He and I didn't get along too well, probably because he was older than I, and he couldn't deal with being subordinate to anybody much younger than he. While I was away training in Tae Kwon Do, he ignored an order from our commander to put in my pay voucher. I got back on a Saturday night and, no pay. I hunted up the sergeant. When I found him he appeared to have gotten an early start on his Saturday night festivities. "Didn't you put in my pay voucher?" I asked.

"No. Why should I?" he asked insolently. "Are you too much of a big shot to do it yourself?" He tried to drive his point home by throwing a punch at me. Now, striking a superior officer is a major offense, a thing you simply don't do in any army, especially when that officer is freshly back from training in the martial arts. I blocked his punch and countered with one of my own. He toppled backward, sitting hard on the barracks floor. He rose to his feet and glared at me. Then he grabbed an M1 rifle from the rack and began to point it in my direction. It didn't matter whether or not it was loaded. Every soldier is taught right from the first moment he lays hands on a weapon that you do not point it at a person unless you're ready to shoot. I struck the weapon from his hands with a kick. Then I put him down for the count. Fortunately for him, our commanding officer decided not to press charges, and the sergeant major was transferred out to another outfit.

By 1956 I was first lieutenant. Now my officer's pay was enough to send bigger allotments home to assist my mother – a better life for both of us. With the war just a sad memory, and with a steady income, my road now seemed to be an easier one. As first Lieutenant, I was second in command of the unit. In addition to my responsibilities for the various construction projects undertaken, I had a lot of administrative responsibility ranging from personnel issues to procurement of supplies, and the job of taking over whenever the commanding officer was absent.

Officer Training graduation

On leave in Seoul

Around this time I lost my cousin. With his days of guerrilla warfare in the past, he and his friends had turned to more peaceful pursuits. They opened a factory to process rice. The machinery was all powered by a single electric motor turning the main drive shaft with a large belt. One day he saw the belt beginning to slip off the pulley, and tried to push it back into place while the motor was still running. The belt caught his clothing and whipped him upward jamming him against the flywheel. It crushed his chest and he died shortly thereafter.

Through all these times, good and bad, I've always had this fascination over the English language. Most of the English I know has been self taught, but I did get a chance to audit a course in Advanced English that Maryland University put on at the Yong San base in Korea, and another course put on there by Los Angeles college. This was the first and only formal teaching of English I had before coming to America.

There came another important milestone on my road. I had a friend at the church I attended, a college student, who one day invited me to his home and introduced me to his family. When his mother learned that I was a single fellow, she wanted me to meet her cousin. She didn't conceal the fact that she had marriage on her mind. The cousin lived about ten miles outside of town. We went to the cousin's house, and there I met Jung Sun. She was a very pretty country girl. We got along well right from the start. After that we dated a few times. She would come to her cousin's house and we would go out to dinner or to a movie, and sometimes to a church function. We started to feel serious about each other.

Of course, like any young man, I sometimes doubted my feelings. Through all the windings of my road, through all the frightening experiences I had endured, there had never been anything quite like this. It was a different way of being scared. I worried about the silliest things – things like the differences in education. Education was still hard to obtain in Korea in those days. I had a good education; Jung Sung did not. Would that difference become a stumbling block in our relationship, or was I making too much of a small thing? Custom prevailed and I discussed my concerns with my mother.

We were married in the traditional Korean way.

Mother had the right answer. She had had a dream the night before. In her dream she foresaw a better life for all of us. She knew it would be a good marriage, and she told me so. Jung Sun's mother also approved and we were married a month or so later with a Korean-style wedding. My mother was right. Married life has been good to both of us. It wasn't long before I looked lovingly into the eyes of my first son, but for my mother, it was a different story.

There are times when, no matter how hard you try to do the right thing, it just doesn't work. When Jung Sun and I were married I rented a house with two bedrooms, one for Jung Sun and me, the other for my mother. However, my mother was of a different generation than my wife, and the generation gap seemed to grow wider as time went on. At first, I did not realize how serious the problems were, but I found out the hard way.

It happened after we'd been married about four years. By then I was out of the army, working as a civilian fire fighter on the U.S. base in Seoul. When I arrived home from work one day, I found my mother in a deep sleep, and an empty medicine bottle beside her bed. I rushed her to the hospital just in time to save her life. There it was determined that she had taken an overdose of sleeping pills.

I was stunned. I kept asking myself, "Why?" My mother had always been so strong. She had gone through so much. She had held up so well through the flight from P'unggi, then from Taegu. She had made her way back to P'unggi alone over a hundred miles. She had been a tower of strength when my younger brother lay dying of TB. She had hung in there like a champion through the postwar years. Why would she try to kill herself now when the worst of the bad times were far behind her and so much promise lay ahead? Then I began to discover what had been going on.

The friction with Jung Sun had gotten to her. It seems my mother had actually felt that I would be happier if she could die and thereby end the strife between her and my wife. Once she was out of the hospital, Jung Sun and I did our best to avoid conflicts between them. My mother regained her strength and finally she and I had a talk. "Son," she said, "I think it would be best for all of us if I moved out of your house." She moved back to P'unggi in 1964 to live with my sister and my elder brother. I felt badly over this for a long time afterward.

Chapter 9

Civilian Life

I was retired from the ROK army in 1963. I had enough severance pay to buy a house near Seoul, close to the Kimpo International Airport. This was a vast improvement over the home I'd grown up in back in P'unggi. Electric lighting and refrigeration were now far more commonplace than just a few years before. No more thatch on the roof. Conventional roofing worked much better – less maintenance, although it couldn't beat thatch for insulating qualities.

The heating was a modern evolution of the system used back in P'unggi. The main heater, which served both for heating the house and for cooking, was still set in a depression in the kitchen, but with many improvements. No longer did we use a wood fire, but an ingenious kind of coal-burning furnace. It consisted of three cylindrical pieces stacked one atop the other. Each cylinder contained a fuel pellet made of a mixture of coal dust and clay, perforated to allow air circulation. Once ignited, the fuel would burn from the bottom upward, eventually igniting the fuel in next higher cylinder. Then the burned-out cylinder would be emptied of ash, recharged, and placed on the top of the stack. In this way a constant fire was maintained. Finally, instead of circulating the smoke beneath the floor as had been done years ago, water was circulated through a water jacket around the heater, then through pipes in the floor. Since the source of the heat was at the lowest point in the system, the water circulated by natural convection; no pump was needed. It was a simple system, but effective.

All of Korea had undergone tremendous changes. The Korea I had known as a child was, for the most part, a nostalgic memory, brought to an abrupt end by the war that had swept back and forth over the land like a tsunami, ending forever much of the gentle ways we had once known. But what was an end for many turned out to be a new beginning for those who survived. A whole new economy together with new ideas and new lifestyles were rapidly becoming part of a new Korea.

By then I had children to support. Once we were settled into our new home, Jung Sun suggested that I try to find a job with the U.S. Army. "You are fluent in English," she said, "and you've acquired a good understanding of engineering while you were in the Korean Army." This made a lot of sense, so the next day found me at the gate of the 76th Engineering Battalion. This group had often interacted with my unit in some of the rebuilding projects, and I at least knew the name of their commanding officer.

Getting in to see the officer was a bit difficult. The guard at the gate wanted to turn me away. "You can't just walk in and see the colonel just like that," he said. "You need to make an appointment."

"This is rather important," I answered. "May I speak with your sergeant?" He called his sergeant and I repeated my request. "I know him from my service in the Korean Army," I explained, "and this will only take a few minutes."

The sergeant then called his commander. When he hung up the phone he instructed me to follow him. He conducted me to the door of the commander's office; I knocked and went in. I introduced myself to the commander, and asked his assistance in contacting the personnel office so that I could apply for work. The colonel called the personnel office at Pu Pyong, then told me to go there. "The personnel director will wait for you until 10:00 AM," he said. I thanked the colonel, then I hitched a ride on a passing truck and was at the personnel office in just a few minutes.

At the personnel office, the guard tried to turn me away until I dropped the colonel's name. Then I was immediately admitted. The personnel director interviewed me, then told me there was an opening for a fire inspector with the 83rd Ordinance Battalion at Shi Hung. "But first," she said, "you'll have to pass a competitive exam."

The exam was given a few days after that. Again, my English helped out, and several days later, I received a letter informing me that I had passed the exam with a high score, and had won the job. Even after having passed the exam, there was still a lot of study required of me. I had to become familiar with the fire codes and the fire-safety regulations peculiar to the base. As a fire inspector, I was responsible for seeing to the compliance to the codes in the two thousand or so buildings, large or small, that were on the base. I would look for fire hazards, and see that fire extinguishers or other fire-fighting equipment was in place and operational. There was a regular schedule of inspections, and the various units had a week or two advance notice to get everything in order.

We also conducted instruction classes in the use of the different kinds of fire extinguishers – which one was best for what kind of fire, and we gave fire-prevention instruction both to adults on the base and to their children in the school.

It was a job that required a lot of diplomacy. This is true in any kind of a quality-assurance situation. One can easily make enemies when discovering and reporting shortcomings in meeting the required safety standards. All the same, if a fire occurred and was traced to fire-safety violations that I had overlooked or failed to report, I could be in a lot of trouble. I had to be very discreet in the way I related to the people I was working with, keeping my focus on getting problems corrected without making any more waves than necessary. This was brought home to me in a very real way when faulty wiring caused a fire in the golf-club kitchen. In the investigation that followed, my reports on inspections of the facility over the previous few months were closely scrutinized. Fortunately, nothing was found that could reflect back on me.

Two years later, there was a downsizing in U.S. forces and my position as fire inspector was phased out. I had a couple months warning, and learned of an opening for a fire fighter in the base's main fire station. This meant some more training courses, but I got through them. It was a different situation; my previous job had been a daytime position, but now I was on 24-hour shifts. The job as fire inspector had been relatively safe; this one was not. As a fireman I frequently found myself in harm's way. Fighting a fire is not unlike fighting a war. One can get killed either way. In a war, however, the enemy has a mind. A fire does not have a mind, and it can be entirely unpredictable. Also, handling a fire hose is a technique all in itself. Think of it this way. When you fire a rifle, it has a momentary recoil; a fire hose delivering large volumes of water under high pressure has a continuous recoil. If you lose control, the hose will escape from your grip and whip around like an enormous, angry snake with the force of a kicking mule – very dangerous and difficult to regain control.

Our training and our equipment all came from the United States, and among the civilian fire fighters, just as there was in military ranks, there was one person who always seemed to know where to get whatever was needed by hook or by crook. Like the army officer we used to call "The Big Fish," he took care of his own people, especially when doing so was to his own advantage. In his job, he was continuously on the move, from one fire station to another. He always knew where to dig up surplus hose, fire-fighting supplies, and equipment, and he always knew where it was most advantageously disposed of. He took good care of us, but he took even better care of himself. In America, such a person is sometimes called a weasel.

While the base fire department was primarily intended to respond to calls within the base, we would go off base if there was an emergency and we were asked to do so. One such emergency was a large fire in a commercial building in Seoul. We arrived to find the building (five or six stories) burning on the bottom floor, which was a market. There were people inside. Our first priority was to get the people out, then fight the fire. The fire was in the back of the building – a lucky break. At least the main entrance and stairs were still usable, but the building was filled with smoke.

We donned our breathing masks, entered the building and began checking for victims, room by room. Visibility was almost nonexistent. I got up to the third floor, and there I could barely make out the forms of bodies on the floor. I yelled to my companions, at the same time lifting the first person onto my shoulders. I got him out, then went back for more. In and out, in and out, I didn't bother counting how many. In this kind of a game, you don't have time to keep score.

We got most of the people out, but the fire was spreading too fast for us to get them all. Our team had its first casualty; the assistant chief was killed by falling debris. By then I was holding a hose, while looking up at a fifty-foot wall that was fully involved in fire, and likely to collapse at any moment. It was a stubborn fire that took a long time to get under control. We lost track of the time. I've no idea what time it was when we finally got back onto the base. We were all dead tired and dealing with the loss of our assistant chief, but we still had to get ourselves and our equipment cleaned up and ready for the next call before falling, exhausted, onto our cots.

We were not lacking work on the base. A military base is in many ways comparable to a city, and like any city fire department, we were kept busy. When not responding to an actual fire, we were constantly maintaining the fire equipment, our building and the grounds.

It was dangerous work. Sometimes a wall would collapse, or a floor cave in. Often we had to rescue one or more people. There were several calls that I remember especially – a commissary building, a warehouse, and a kitchen fire in an apartment building. We had to carry a couple of unconscious people out. I earned several citations for my rescue work. They were to prove very valuable later on when I applied to come to America.

I remained a fireman for five years. Then I was upgraded to communications officer. This was also shift work, but it was an eight-hour shift, rather than 24 hours. In that capacity I received incoming alarms, dispatched fire fighting crews to the alarm scenes, then monitored their progress by radio so that needs for extra personnel or equipment could be immediately met. I also had to keep the higher command aware of its progress. Seven years later I had the opportunity to again become a fire inspector, and I remained in that job until I retired.

I had also remained active with my church, and had been ordained an elder. In that capacity, I assisted with religious services on the base every Wednesday evening, and on Sunday.

My older brother was in his 40's when I married, still working very hard to care for his family, but his drinking problem had caught up with him. He eventually developed stomach cancer. I wanted to help with his medical expenses, possibly even pay for surgery, but there was no point in that. It was already too late. A cousin of mine, who was a nurse, advised me that even with surgery, he had not long to live, a few months at the most. He died shortly after that, leaving his two sons in my mother's care. Four years later, at the age of 74, my mother passed away. She lies on a hillside just outside of P'unggi close to her sons.

About six years after my mother died, I learned from a family member that my eldest brother was still alive and living in Manchuria. I inquired through the postal service, and they were able to find his address. I got in touch with him, and one thing led to another. We obtained a visa so that he could come for a visit. He was with us about three months, renewing contact with old friends and relatives, but the saddest part of his visit was when I took him to our mother's and brother's graves. He broke down completely at our mother's grave site, blaming himself for much of the grief my mother had felt over him. He died five years after the visit.

My oldest sister was married to the owner of a bicycle shop in P'unggi. She died around the time the second world war ended. Another sister had married a farmer during the second world war to avoid being conscripted by the Japanese as a sex slave for their army. Her marriage was a good one, however. She had four children and lived to the age of 75.

Chapter 10

The American Dream

South Korea has undergone a tremendous transformation since the end of World War II and the Korean war. We have made the transition from near third-world status to becoming a significant factor in the world's economy. The mud-and-bamboo huts of my childhood are now just a dim memory. Jung Sun and I lived on the outskirts of Seoul, enjoying all the benefits of the twentieth century. My children had a far more promising future than anything I had ever known, but even better things were in store for the next generation.

When I retired from my firefighting career in 1992, there was a benefit available to civilian employees who were retiring with more than fifteen years of outstanding service. Persons who qualified could apply for permanent residency in the United States. With thirty years of service, along with many commendations I had received in my firefighting career, I applied for admission into this country with the warm approval of the base commander. At the same time, I opened an account with the Bank of the United States, and began building up funds in anticipation of moving. It took two years for all the red tape to run out, but one fine day, the mail delivered a visa for permanent residence for myself, my wife, and my youngest son. The four older sons, being over 21, had to remain in Korea.

Once the visa arrived, it took another two months to get ready. It was a busy time. I had to dispose of everything I couldn't take with me. I had to pack and ship everything else. I had to make arrangements for our arrival here. With the aid of a friend in this country, I reserved a two-bedroom apartment in Federal way, Washington.

Finally, on October 23, 1995, we boarded an airplane for the nine-hour flight to Sea-Tac airport. It was with mixed feelings that I watched through the window of the airplane as it left the ground. I was leaving the homeland I had known all my life. All at the same time I felt a deep sadness over what

I was leaving and was filled with anticipation of what lay ahead.

We stayed the first two weeks with our friend, while we set about furnishing our apartment and providing all the little things that make an apartment into a home. It was a happy day when we finally moved into our own apartment. After the months of preparation, the flight to the U.S., and the weeks of furnishing and setting up our new home, I could finally relax in my own home, and think about what to do next. Once we were settled, I got a job at the local Top Food Store doing maintenance work. Then I could finally spend some time exploring my new homeland.

There is always some amount of wonder in first discovery. While Seoul is every bit as modern a city as Seattle, each city is different in its own way, and everywhere we turned there was something new to see. We took in all the attractions of the city and the neighboring countryside with every bit as much delight as little children going to a circus.

My son and I both registered to take classes at Highline Community College, where I continued to pursue my study of the English language. I attended four years at Highline, then had a year at Edmonds Community College, followed by 3 more years at Everett community College.

I also did some volunteer work for the Federal Way fire department. I was in a unique position for that. The Seattle area has a very large Korean population, many of whom are still struggling to learn the English language. With my experience as a fire fighter and my understanding of fire-prevention methods, I was able to conduct fire-safety classes for these people in their own language, a thing that they greatly appreciated.

I received full citizenship on Independence Day 2001; My wife and youngest son received their citizenship the next year. There remained my four sons in Korea, and while my own citizenship was in process, I had begun the necessary paperwork to bring them here. Now two of them are here, and the remaining two are close to approval. The youngest son, while still a U.S. citizen, is presently working in Thailand

Back in Korea, I had two thirteen-year-old twin grand daughters. Their father wanted them to have their education in this country. I began inquiring into the immigration laws to determine the best way to accomplish this. It turned out that the easiest way for me to keep the children in this country was by legally adopting them. My son was agreeable to this, so my wife flew to Korea and brought the girls back on a travel visa. It took the aid of an attorney to complete the adoption process. Once the adoption was final, the travel visa was extended until the girls could receive permanent residence status. They have since gone through college, and become contributing members of the American society. Three more grandchildren have come here in the same way, and are presently living with me.

When I look back at all this, I am sometimes amazed at the way everything has turned out. Right from the very beginning I have always had this burning desire to reach out, to learn other languages. At first it was Japanese. Then, when the GI's came, I somehow felt that learning their language would be the key to a better life. It has been proven so. Had I not been able to read and understand English, I could not have taken the officer training courses, as all the textbooks had come from the U.S. and were in English. Then the training in fire fighting for my eventual civilian job also required a knowledge of English. Once in this country, my knowledge of Korean made it possible for me to assist the local fire fighters in their efforts to educate my countrymen in fire safety. In this way I could give back some of the training here in America that had been given to me by America so long ago.

Finally my understanding of the language was essential in filling out the immigration paperwork, not only for myself but for my children and grandchildren. Except for the adoption process, I accomplished all this without the aid of a lawyer, thanks again to a knowledge of the language. I managed to do all the necessary paperwork myself, and in doing so learned enough about the immigration system to have it work for me instead of against me. However faulty my spoken and written English may seem, it has served me well – very well indeed.

I have come a long way from being the child that my father carried each day to the rice paddy, to being the man that I am now. The road has been long, sometimes rough, sometimes even dangerous, but each rough place, each unexpected turn, be they good or bad, has served one way or another to move me closer to the good life I now have. It may have been well that I could never see beyond the next turn, for if I could, the road ahead would have been frightening.

There now remains alive only myself and one sister of what had been a family of nine children. Often I have wondered why it was that I survived when all my brothers did not. It may have been that I was just lucky. Perhaps I may have learned enough from seeing the mistakes of others to have determined not to make those same mistakes myself. Perhaps it was a combination of the two. However it may have been, it appears as though a Higher Being has looked down upon us with favor. In His tender mercy and, for reasons I do not know, He has seen fit to bring me and my progeny into this good land, and for them, the road ahead is filled with promises of better times to come.

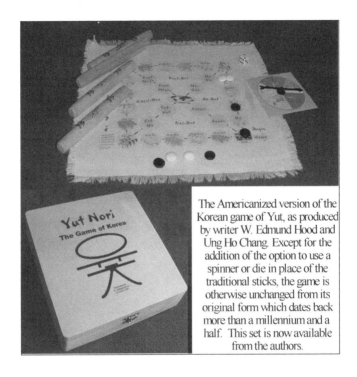

The Americanized version of the Korean game of Yut, as produced by writer W. Edmund Hood and Ung Ho Chang. Except for the addition of the option to use a spinner or die in place of the traditional sticks, the game is otherwise unchanged from its original form which dates back more than a millennium and a half. This set is now available from the authors.

Send $29.95 plus $5.00 shipping & handling to:

W. Edmund Hood
227 97th Street SE
Everett WA 98208

In Washington State, add State Sales Tax.

sons of Korah
Jackals
gold from Ophir
Tyre